THEODORE ROOSEVELT

A Life From Beginning to End

Copyright © 2016 by Hourly History Limited

Table of Contents

Introduction

There's nothing like a political assassination to change the course of history. Where once there was someone in charge, suddenly they are gone - and someone else needs to take their place. Oftentimes, the results are mixed. After all, who can stand center-stage, pick up the pieces so to speak, and manage to be so influential?

In such a situation, it requires someone young and invigorating, someone who has filled their resume with lots of things prior to taking the oath of office for President of the United States. Someone poised on the edge of a new century, a modern century. Someone who has the capacity to change the course of American history.

That someone was Theodore Roosevelt. "Teedie", as he was called as a boy, grew up to have an incredible life. He was a man perfectly suited to his times; one who moved in conjunction with the political winds of the day.

There is so much to know about this modern man. Youngest of any man to hold the esteemed office of President of the United States, Roosevelt knew how to use his charm and what seemed like his superhuman energy to rally a nation to ever exceptional heights of greatness. From building the Panama Canal to winning the Nobel Prize to creating his Rough Riders and journeying down the Amazon River, there seems as if there was nothing this man couldn't do.

Husband, father, assemblyman, cowboy, police commissioner, National Guardsman, governor, vice president, president, safari hunter; Theodore Roosevelt filled all these roles. Never one to sit still for very long, Roosevelt never let anything stand in his way. His policies changed the face of American politics for all time.

The following is an in-depth look at one of the most interesting public figures in all of American history - someone who would have been be quite at home in 21st-century America and a man who has consistently been ranked as one of this country's greatest presidents.

Chapter One

Early Life & Education

"With self-discipline, most anything is possible."

—Theodore Roosevelt

Theodore Roosevelt was a far cry a log-cabin president. Indeed, you might have had some problem finding a log cabin in Manhattan, New York, but that's where Roosevelt was born. It was October 27, 1858, just a few years away from a bloody civil war that would tear the United States apart.

Theodore Roosevelt was born in a four-story brownstone on East 20th Street in NYC. His mother Martha Stewart "Mittie" Bulloch was a socialite; his father Theodore Roosevelt Sr. was a businessman. Theodore was the second of four children and they were all born into a wealthy family.

There were no money problems for young Theodore. However, all through his childhood he did suffer from respiratory problems, mostly asthma. He would usually wake up in the middle of the night with a severe asthma attack, feeling as if he were being smothered to death. There was no cure and it scared him tremendously.

Possibly to keep the asthma demons at bay, Theodore Roosevelt became interested in just about everything in his world. He had a lifelong passion for zoology which began in childhood. Being naturally inquisitive and always wanting answers to everything, Theodore embraced a strenuous lifestyle.

Along with two of his cousins, young Theodore formed a "Roosevelt Museum of Natural History" where the three of them would study dead animals and insects that they collected. He even had his own basic taxidermy kit. Rather than merely learning knowledge from books, Theodore loved doing things which brought him knowledge of the world long before he was a part of it.

Theodore Roosevelt Sr. was a great influence on his son. He was already a well-known leader in New York City cultural affairs and helped to found the Metropolitan Museum of Art. Theodore Sr. expected certain behavior from all four of his children and would not tolerate any selfishness, cruelty, idleness or untruthfulness.

When he was about eleven years old, Theodore visited Europe with his family. There he went hiking in the Alps in 1869. Even at a young age, Roosevelt found he could keep up with his father. It was then that he discerned that a healthy lifestyle could be achieved through hard physical exercise. So Roosevelt began a strenuous exercise regimen; not only did he learn how to box, but he found that his asthma was greatly reduced with physical play.

It was during his childhood that Theodore Roosevelt was influenced by great and courageous men, some of whom he knew through his studies and others, like his father, who were close by. From reading about the adventures of early Americans during the Revolutionary

War and from hearing the stories of his own ancestors, Roosevelt saw how fearless these men were, how they could hold their own in the world and how it made them each successful in their own ways. He determined that he wanted to be that kind of a man.

Theodore Roosevelt Sr. had a fourth cousin, James Roosevelt I, who was a businessman like many in the family. James was also the father of Franklin Delano Roosevelt, who would go on to be the 32nd president of the United States.

Education

Even though Theodore Roosevelt came from a prominent, wealthy family, he was home schooled by his parents and tutors. "Teedie" Roosevelt as Theodore was called by family and friends (how the "Teddy" bear came to symbolize his name is something you'll read in a later chapter) had an uneven education. He loved subjects such as geography, history and languages but didn't do so well in mathematics, Latin or Greek.

In 1876, Roosevelt enrolled in Harvard College. Two years into his studies in 1878, Theodore's father died. He was quite devastated over the loss of his father, and once he was back at school he threw himself into his studies.

During this time Roosevelt excelled in just about every course he took. Being drawn to the natural world, he studied biology and other sciences; he also did well in philosophy and rhetoric. Theodore graduated from Harvard in 1880 magna cum laude.

After graduation, Roosevelt entered Columbia Law School in NYC but quickly became disenchanted with law. He was also busy at this time writing a book about the War of 1812 and decided to run for public office. Friends he knew encouraged him to this new path; so he dropped out of law school and devoted himself to becoming a member of the governing class.

Sagamore Hill

When he was 22 years old, Roosevelt bought 155 acres of land on the North Shore of Long Island at Cove Neck, about 2 miles from Oyster Bay. It was here that Roosevelt had spent many childhood summers with his family growing up; this area held numerous special memories for him.

In 1884 Theodore hired an architectural firm to design and build a Queen Anne-style home on the property. It took two years to complete building the 22-room house and Roosevelt moved in the following year.

The house and the farmland that surrounds it were the primary residence for Theodore and Edith Roosevelt for the rest of their lives. It became known as the "Summer White House" during the seven years that Roosevelt was president.

In 1962, Sagamore Hill was made a National Historic Site as part of the National Park Service which Theodore had established during his presidency. As with many other presidential homes, you can visit Sagamore Hill as it is open to the public for tours.

Chapter Two

Early Political Career and Marriage

"It is hard to fail, but it is worse never to have tried to succeed"

—Theodore Roosevelt

Theodore Roosevelt was soon on his way to political endeavors. In 1882 he was elected to the New York Assembly for the Republicans. Again in 1883 and 1884 he was an assemblyman. Immediately he began fighting corruption issues of the day.

The late 19th century was a time of great upheaval in not only America but also the world. New inventions such as the railroad, the discovery of oil and factories fueled by the Industrial Revolution had made multi-millionaires out of many ordinary citizens who had just happened to be in the right place at the right time. These families would go on to influence American politics for generations.

Political corruption was no different back in those days than it is today. Roosevelt was able to expose potential corruption in Albany, New York's state capital, through investigations that he had started. He also ended up writing more bills than any other legislator at the time.

By the time of the presidential election of 1884, Roosevelt supported a bland character named George Edmunds, a senator from Vermont. The current president, fellow New Yorker Chester Arthur, had fallen out of favor with Roosevelt.

However, Roosevelt attended the GOP convention that year in Chicago, where he addressed a crowd of over ten thousand people, the largest such group he had yet spoken to. Theodore felt he was drawn more to national politics than to state elections. With that he withdrew to his new abode, which he had christened "Chimney Butte Ranch", on the Little Missouri in North Dakota to think about his future.

When he established his two ranches in the Badlands of western North Dakota, Roosevelt had never owned one acre of land. He was a squatter like every other rancher in the territory. Land at that time still belonged to the NP Railroad. The Chimney Butte Ranch was also known as the Maltese Cross.

On his 22nd birthday, Theodore Roosevelt married Alice Hathaway Lee, daughter of a wealthy banker and his wife. Their daughter Alice Lee Roosevelt was born on February 12, 1884.

Two days after giving birth to her daughter, on Valentine's Day, Alice Hathaway Lee died from undiagnosed kidney complications. In his diary, Theodore Roosevelt placed a large "X" on that page, and noted that the "light has gone out of my life."

Unbelievably on this same day, his mother Mittie had died hours earlier of typhoid fever. Both his mother and his wife died the same day in the same house. Theodore Roosevelt was distraught to say the least. Roosevelt left his new baby Alice in the care of his sister Bamie in New York City while he took time to grieve. It wasn't until Alice was three years old that Theodore would regain custody of his daughter.

Theodore Roosevelt headed west. A new widower, he didn't want to stay where memories of his wife were all around him. It was better to be far away from what he had known in New York City with his wife Alice, and new baby daughter.

Roosevelt "retired" to his ranch here to grieve over the loss of his wife and mother. For the rest of his life, Roosevelt rarely spoke of his wife Alice and did not include her in his autobiography. Even later on in his life, Roosevelt, while working on a biography, never mentioned either of his wives while going through his papers.

Chapter Three

The Old West and a New Beginning

"I have always said I would not have been President had it not been for my experience in North Dakota."

—Theodore Roosevelt

A young man and a widower was the situation Theodore Roosevelt found himself in 1884. Alone and grieving, he went to North Dakota which was still classified as a territory at that time. Here Theodore built a second ranch named Elk Horn, which is still today one of the most beautiful and isolated places in the Badlands.

It was here that Roosevelt played cowboy. He learned how to ride a horse western-style, how to rope and lasso, and how to hunt. He started writing about his experiences for several magazines. Roosevelt also became a deputy sheriff and captured some bad guys. Once while pursuing some horse thieves he made the acquaintance of Seth Bullock, who was the sheriff of Deadwood, South Dakota. The two would remain lifelong friends.

Theodore Roosevelt's future philosophies were formed during these years. He believed men should pursue manly endeavors and leave off all what he called "pseudo-philanthropists." Manly qualities, he believed, were vital to the strength of a nation. How right he would be.

The Elkhorn Ranch cabin, which is today long gone, was quite luxurious for the place it was in. You can still view the 60 x 30 foot cabin foundation stones if you visit there today. The surrounding countryside is much like it was in Theodore Roosevelt's time. Roosevelt would ranch and hunt here and often go on solo horseback rides, sometimes for days at a time.

While at his two ranches in North Dakota, Roosevelt led successful efforts to address the problems of overgrazing and other conservation efforts. When the severe winter of 1886-1887 wiped out his herd, and most of his money, Roosevelt returned to New York City.

By 1886, Roosevelt married for the second time. Edith Kermit Carow was a long-time family friend, and they were married in London, England. One of Edith's grandfather's had been a Union general in the Civil War. Edith grew up next door to Teddy Roosevelt, so she knew him and his family.

The couple went to Europe for their 15-week honeymoon tour. They returned home to Sagamore Hill and in time ended up having five children: Theodore "Ted III", Kermit, Ethel, Archibald and Quentin.

This marriage would serve Theodore well; Edith was with him until the end of his days. Edith would live until September 30, 1948, dying at the age of 87.

Chapter Four

Early Public Life

"Character, in the long run, is the decisive factor in the life of an individual and of nations alike."

—Theodore Roosevelt

The United States in the late 1880s was a vastly different place from what it was before the Civil War. New inventions such as the telephone and electricity were coming into cultural life, and once the war ended there was an influx of immigrants who seemed to pour continuously in to the country.

Most were from Europe; some Irish and German immigrants had come before the war, but now it seemed as if the flood gates had been opened. People were drawn to the United States for all it offered and for people who hoped for a better life for themselves and their children.

Industrialists such as John D. Rockefeller (oil), Andrew Carnegie (steel), Cornelius Vanderbilt (water transport, railroads), Jay Gould (railroads), J.P. Morgan (finance, industrial consolidation), and John Jacob Astor (real estate, fur) were the new movers and shakers in these last decades of the 19th century. Most, if not all, of these businessmen became fabulously wealthy through unethical business practices. They rigged the markets, crushed their competitors, and corrupted government all for power and money. They sold their goods to an unwitting public who could get rich themselves on the coattails of these men.

It was into this convoluted world of business and politics that Theodore Roosevelt stepped back into in 1888.

Chapter Five

Becoming a National Figure

"The most successful politician is he who says what the people are thinking most often in the loudest voice."

—Theodore Roosevelt

1888, Theodore Roosevelt emerged from his self-imposed retirement. This time around, he endorsed a winner for president: Benjamin Harrison. For his efforts Roosevelt was appointed the U.S. Civil Service Commissioner until 1895. He prudently enforced all civil service laws and took his job seriously.

During the presidential election of 1892, Roosevelt again endorsed Harrison, but he was not re-elected. Instead the new president, Grover Cleveland, reappointed Roosevelt to the Civil Service post. All during his tenure as civil service commissioner, Roosevelt fought the "spoils system" or what we know today as patronage.

Newly elected officials were very used to giving government jobs to family, friends and anyone who supported them when they ran for office. This is very much against government regulation, yet it ran rampant in the 1880s and 1890s. However, with Roosevelt's help much of this activity was quashed.

Then in 1894 Roosevelt was approached by fellow Republicans and asked to become mayor of New York

City. His wife didn't want to leave the Washington D.C. social set and so Theodore refused the offer to his regret. Immediately he realized this was an opportune way of getting back into politics.

Within the year, Roosevelt became president of the board of the New York City Police Commissioners. At this time, in 1895, the NYPD was known around the world as one of the most corrupt police forces, but under Roosevelt's watch this would change radically.

He set out to reform and eradicate any and all of corruption he saw. Annual physical exams were required and regular firearm inspections were implemented; he hired new recruits, most of whom were not affiliated with any particular political party; he had many of the meeting rooms where corrupt cops would gather closed permanently. Telephones were also installed in all police stations.

As police commissioner, Roosevelt would walk police beats late at night and into the early morning hours to check on officers to see if they were really on the job. Eventually all of his "meddling" would result in the board of police commissioners being legislated out of existence. It wouldn't be until Roosevelt was governor of New York State that he would sign legislation replacing the board of police commissioners with a single police commissioner.

In 1897, Roosevelt became the Assistant Secretary of the Navy. As a result of his reputation, most major decisions in this position were left up to him. President McKinley knew how passionate Roosevelt was about history and Theodore didn't let him down.

Spanish-American War

It turned out there was a little problem with Cuba. Spain was interfering in this island country. Roosevelt reminded President McKinley that according to the Monroe Doctrine, which had been implemented in 1823, that no European nation could be permitted to interfere in states or lands in North or South America; it would be viewed as an aggression that the U.S. would have to address.

Once it seemed that war would be inevitable between the U.S. and Spain, Roosevelt took matters into his own hands. As he served as acting Secretary of the Navy, he readied the U.S. Navy for war by ordering ammunition and supplies. The coming conflict would become known to be the Spanish-American War.

In April 1898, Roosevelt formed the First US Cavalry Regiment when America and Spain declared war on one another. This particular unit was only active for the duration of the Spanish-American War, and was known as the "Rough Riders." There were many different types of people who made up the Rough Riders: professional and amateur athletes, Ivy League students, Native Americans, hunters, cowboys, former soldiers, miners, sheriffs, and men of considerable wealth.

In mid-June of 1898, Roosevelt and his regiment left Florida and landed in Cuba where they had a short, minor skirmish fighting off the Spanish resistance. On July 1, 1898 came the Battle of San Juan Hill, the most famous battle of the Spanish-American War; under Roosevelt's command the Rough Riders became famous for their charge up Kettle Hill. San Juan Hill and Kettle Hill were decisive victories for the Americans but came at great cost: casualties included 200 killed and 1000 wounded.

Roosevelt had ridden back and forth between the rifle pits at Kettle Hill during the conflict, urging his soldiers forward. Pinned down by enemy fire, Roosevelt believed there was only one thing to do. Accompanied by four or five men, he led a charge up San Juan Hill in total disregard for his life.

Theodore Roosevelt later in his life recalled the Battle of Kettle Hill as "the greatest day of my life". Colonel Roosevelt, as he preferred being called, was awarded the Medal of Honor posthumously for his deeds in that battle by President Bill Clinton in 2001. There are some who argued that Roosevelt was denied the medal during his lifetime because he had opposed higher authorities. Others believed Roosevelt had exaggerated his role in the fighting. Either way, he is the only American president to have ever received a Medal of Honor.

It was from this point onward that the American public started referring to Roosevelt as "Teddy". He much preferred being called Colonel Roosevelt or The Colonel, but the public always referred to him as Teddy, much to his dislike.

Chapter Six

Governor and Vice President

"There has never yet been a man in our history who led a life of ease whose name is worth remembering."

—Theodore Roosevelt

As the 19ᵗʰ century was coming to its end, Roosevelt returned home after leaving the Army. New York Republicans approached him asking that he run for governor of the state, as the current governor was riddled by scandal. In 1898, Roosevelt won easily on his war record.

As governor of New York, Theodore began learning the ropes of economics and politics that would serve him well in the years ahead. One of the keys to his success was that Roosevelt held twice-daily press conferences and remained connected to the new and ever-growing middle class in the state. Remember, at this time immigrants were flooding into Ellis Island by the thousands each year; these people were drawn to the U.S. for a better life.

There were many issues at hand that Roosevelt would deal with as governor. He learned firsthand about trusts, monopolies, labor relations and the power of the federal government. This was the era of large corporations seemingly taking over public life in America. It seemed whatever they wanted all these corporations had to do was to bribe the government and it was granted to them.

Theodore Roosevelt recognized the power of these businesses. Trying to get any reform passed is usually a game played with the political bosses of the day, and it was no different at the turn of the century. However, Roosevelt successfully passed much legislation even without their approval. It was during his tenure as governor of New York that Roosevelt would develop many of the principles that would shape his presidency. His belief in public advocacy of large corporations, regulation of railroads, mediation that would take place between government and the labor force, and conservation of natural resources were all aspects that had their beginnings in a Roosevelt governorship.

By November of 1899, as Theodore Roosevelt was looking forward to a second term as governor of New York, President McKinley's vice-president died of heart failure. Many of Roosevelt's friends believed that a second gubernatorial term would be a dead end for him politically and they supported him to become a candidate for the vice-presidential opening.

New York State was a haven for large corporations. Roosevelt had been adept at reforming legislation where the insurance and franchises businesses were concerned, so, he was no friend of big business at this time. Many friends, as well as enemies, were looking forward to his removal from public office in New York.

President McKinley would not consider him for Secretary of War, but had no problem with Roosevelt becoming the new vice-president. Roosevelt energetically campaigned for McKinley, traveling around the country and telling people that the President deserved re-election as he had brought peace and prosperity to the citizens. The Republicans won in a landslide.

Theodore Roosevelt became our nation's vice-president in March of 1901. He would be in this position for a mere six months until September. There was nothing much to speak about where his vice-presidency was concerned except for one little quote of his: at the Minnesota State Fair he declared: "Speak softly and carry a big stick, and you will go far."

He had used this famous quote the year earlier, but it wasn't until 1901 at a public address that Roosevelt said it again for all the country to hear. It fit in nicely with his foreign policy philosophy of negotiating peacefully but threatening with the "big stick" or military prowess.

Four days later on September 6, 1901, President McKinley was shot twice in the abdomen by an anarchist named Leon Czolgosz. At first it looked as if the President would survive. Surgeons couldn't locate the second bullet though, and seven days later gangrene set in. McKinley took a turn for the worse and died on September 14.

Theodore Roosevelt received news of McKinley's death in North Creek, New York. He immediately rushed to Buffalo, where he was sworn in at the Ansley Wilcox House, now a national monument. Roosevelt was now the nation's 26th President of the United States. He was 42 years old, making him the youngest president ever of the United States. Roosevelt now had his chance at leading the country into what came to be known as the Progressive Era.

Chapter Seven

Presidency

"We can have no '50-50' allegiance in this country. Either a man is an American and nothing else, or he is not an American at all."

—Theodore Roosevelt

By the time the United States was entering the 20th century, it was a far different country than it had been just a hundred years before. Now, immigrants were changing the face of America itself even as local, state and federal governments had grown mostly corrupt and were run by political machines and their bosses. Huge companies such as Standard Oil and others were becoming monopolies, allowing for little to no competition.

But there was a new feel to the country. The horse and buggy was being replaced by the automobile, telephones and telegraphs were keeping people in touch, and the country stretched from one ocean to the other with lots of room in-between - room to make a better life.

This is where Theodore Roosevelt found himself when he took over the presidency. At first, he kept McKinley's cabinet and agreed to abide by his predecessor's policies. In time he would promote progressive policies in their stead, policies which he firmly believed were in the best interests of everyone and not just advantageous to big business. These policies would be an outgrowth of the "Square Deal," a program that he had developed while he had been governor of New York that Roosevelt said rested upon deals being struck by a neutral state.

Square Deal rules were honesty in public affairs, a fair sharing between privilege and responsibility and party and local concerns taking a back seat to the interests of the state at large. During his presidency, Roosevelt dealt with both domestic and foreign policies.

Domestic Affairs

The development of industrial America was due to many factors. Notable among them was the end of Reconstruction, that period in American history where former slaves were to be given all the rights and privileges of any American citizen. Unfortunately, it wouldn't turn out that way until the 1960s. Additionally, the opening of the West was a golden opportunity for citizens and big businesses alike.

Third, immigration kept pace with ever-growing big cities; between 1877 and 1900 foreigners flooded in the country at a rate of about 7 million people in total. They entered every aspect and area of American life. Fourth was the rise of agricultural, commercial and industrial development. This also included transportation methods such as the railroads, which began criss-crossing the entire country. With the American economy bursting at the seams, there were large corporations at the top who seemed to want to direct America's future.

Government was seen as less and less a help to ordinary citizens and more and more a blessing to big business. In response, progressivism became the new movement of the day. It was put into place specifically to correct government corruption and in turn spawned much social activism not seen in the United States since its founding years.

Roosevelt's Square Deal

Theodore Roosevelt's Square Deal was formed upon three basic ideas:

· conservation of natural resources
· control of corporations
· consumer protection

Roosevelt's main aim was to help the middle class. This was the group growing fastest of all with the rise in immigration in the previous decades. Also, at this time, corporations had become monopolies, and many of them turned to the government for their protection.

Much like the more progressively-minded Democrats of today, Roosevelt turned to the government as the cure-all for social evils which would spring up everywhere and anywhere. He denounced big businesses as "representatives of predatory wealth" who usually had no other regard than their own. These companies routinely wanted people to work for low wages with no recourse to remedy their own situations.

One of President Roosevelt's first acts was to curb the power of large corporations, also known as "trusts." Roosevelt brought 40 anti-trust suits against big businesses, trying to break them up. The railroads, especially the great railroad combination in the Northwest, and Standard Oil, which was started by John D. Rockefeller in 1870, were big Roosevelt targets. Standard Oil became the Exxon Corporation in 1972. Roosevelt was also a big supporter of unions. Yet, he backed the gold standard and was supportive of lower taxes overall.

With **railroads** being put down all across the nation, Roosevelt felt it was very important to control railroad rates. He believed that corruption would run rampant when goods and services were shipped over the rails. The best remedy would be government intervention. In 1906 a federal law was created called the Hepburn Act giving the government power to regulate the railroads.

During these years, factories were churning out all manner of products and merchandise for sale to the American people. Many of these facilities were dirty, unregulated and the products made there were fit for no one. Public anger over food packing factories became so strident that these cries traveled all the way to the White House.

The President responded with the Meat Inspection Act of 1906 and the **Pure Food and Drug** Act. No more could companies mislead the public with phony labels and chemical additives. Nothing impure or falsely labeled would be allowed to ship anywhere.

The Pure Food and Drug Act was the first in a long series of consumer protection laws. It eventually led to the creation of the Food and Drug Administration or FDA. Up until this time, packaging of commodities like meat could be done any way a company chose; the new federal law banned mislabeled food and drug products from interstate traffic and shipping.

In 1902 the **coal miners** across the country went on strike. Because most homes and businesses were heated with coal, there was a looming energy shortage. Again, President Roosevelt turned to the government. He threatened to bring federal troops into the mines. A commission was created which arbitrated an end to the strike while at the same time lowering coal prices and closing some coal furnaces.

Many criticized the President for this, as his accord with the coal miners would reduce their working hours but give them more pay, only with no union representation. Roosevelt would always harken back to his Square Deal philosophy: if it wasn't good for every man, it wasn't good for anyone.

In the matter of **business** itself, the Republicans and Roosevelt sought a deal with the bankers in regards to the money supply. The Democrats sought government control and to an extent so did Roosevelt. However, in the end he would side with his Republicans.

As with many modern-day presidents, Roosevelt was not all averse to extending his reach by what we know today as "executive action." He sought executive control in matters of domestic and foreign policy, even if it was not stated so in the Constitution.

Unbelievably, Roosevelt sought to have rules in the game of football changed. He also meddled in the rules and regulations of the Naval Academy, and made changes to a newly minted coin which came out to his dislike. According to friends and foes alike, if Roosevelt saw something he wished to regulate, update or improve, he was all for it.

Of all his domestic policies, Roosevelt was proudest of his conservation achievements. He extended Federal protection to wildlife and land. He established the United States Forest Service, and signed into law five National Parks, which would be the beginnings of the National Parks Service.

Eighteen national monuments were also created, including the Statue of Liberty in New Jersey and New York, the Petrified Forest in Arizona, Devil's Tower in Wyoming, and the Grand Canyon in Arizona. This short list would grow to over one hundred U.S. National Monuments today. Bird and game preserves were also created in addition to National Forests.

When it came to the media, Theodore Roosevelt would have been right at home in our social media driven world. He made it a point to keep news of White House comings and goings front and center all day every day. He used the media daily in press briefings and photo ops. Up until Roosevelt was in office, the reporters used to huddle around outside the White House. One rainy day, Roosevelt invited them in and gave them a room for themselves. Thus, the official White House briefing was born.

Roosevelt was greatly admired by members of the press, and enjoyed very close relationships with many of them. Long before he ever held political office, Theodore Roosevelt had been a writer and editor, and always felt comfortable speaking with authors, writers, and other professionals.

Foreign Policy

There were many areas of the world that needed American attention. In the 1890s Roosevelt had been a big supporter of the acquisition of the Philippines, only to lose interest in this chain of islands after he became president.

He did have a passion for one region of the world and that was the Caribbean, namely Panama. Roosevelt wanted his Panama Canal to be built no matter what. He petitioned Congress to approve a waterway through the Panama isthmus. Roosevelt was aware that there was a strategic need for a waterway which would cut through the tiny neck of land between North and South America. There was a little trouble with the country of Colombia, but by 1903 construction was underway for the Panama Canal to be built. This would become one of Roosevelt's most enduring legacies.

During those early years of the 20th century, there were European rumblings going on in different South American countries. Germany, Italy and England all sought a naval blockade against Venezuela and it was at this time that the "Roosevelt Corollary" was created.

The Roosevelt Corollary was added to the Monroe Doctrine. This doctrine, which had been in place since 1823, stated that any conflicts in North or South America would result in American intervention without being petitioned for aid. Roosevelt's corollary prevented the creation of any foreign bases in the Caribbean and deemed the U.S. the only country with the rights to intervene.

The Corollary stated that the U.S. would intervene any time European nations decided to throw their weight around in Latin American countries. This policy was perfectly in keeping with Roosevelt's Big Stick diplomacy. The United States would exercise police power wherever it chose - and this was something the president endorsed.

Roosevelt was also instrumental in bringing the Russo-Japanese War to an end. For this he received the Nobel Prize. It seems that there was nothing this president couldn't do.

Then in 1906, there was an insurrection in Cuba. Roosevelt sent his Secretary of War, William Howard Taft, to Cuba to oversee the events there. Roosevelt also believed he could direct Taft to send the Marines into Cuba on his own. This would have meant going around Congress; without their approval he would be in violation of the Constitution, as only Congress has the power to declare war.

Election of 1904

In November of 1904, Theodore Roosevelt was elected to a second term, this one won by him in his own right. As you recall, Roosevelt had succeeded President McKinley upon his demise due to assassination. Roosevelt chose Charles W. Fairbanks of Indiana as his running mate. Fairbanks was a conservative Republican with close ties to the railroads.

The Democrats' candidate was one Alton B. Parker, a judge with the New York Court of Appeals. Both candidates held similar political views, believe it or not, and it was just a matter of preference who the American people would deem the better president.

Roosevelt easily defeated Parker, taking every state except for some in the South. Theodore Roosevelt was an immensely popular president in his first term and there was no reason he wouldn't be elected this time.

Over the summer of 1904 Roosevelt conducted his presidential campaign from the back porch of his home in Oyster Bay, Long Island. Neither he nor his running mate ran around the country for months to campaign. It just wasn't done back in those days.

The Great White Fleet

During Roosevelt's second term, from December 1907 to February 1909, the president sent out the United States Navy Battle Fleet for a round-the-world tour for all the world to see. The fleet consisted of 16 battleships, along with other escort vessels.

Roosevelt had one aim in mind: to show the world America's military power and naval capability. The president believed he would be successful at enforcing treaties around the world when these countries saw the strength of the United States passing by. The hulls of these battleships were all painted white, giving this American armada the name "Great White Fleet".

After the Spanish-American War, America had become a major sea power and Roosevelt wanted everyone at home and abroad to recognize this. One of the reasons Roosevelt sent his fleet around the war was to get the attention of Japan. This country had become a major sea power with its defeat of the Russian fleet in 1905.

Roosevelt wanted Tokyo to recognize that America would not be such an easy foe if somehow this was their intention. With American interests in the Pacific and particularly in the Philippines, Roosevelt was assuring American influence anywhere in the world.

At home, because of economic uncertainty with the bank scare of 1907, this 'round-the-world excursion seemed to take people's minds off of their money problems. At the same time it encouraged patriotism.

Up until this point in American naval history, warships like the USS Maine and USS Illinois were designed for coastal reconnaissance. Now with new battleships such as the USS Virginia and USS Connecticut, construction had outfitted these vessels as the first true modern warships – highly appropriate for a new modern century.

One of Roosevelt's predictions was that he would not run again for president once his second term was finished. He thought precedent should be followed. Of course once 1908 came around and he still had unfinished business to attend to, Roosevelt would have liked to stay on for a third term. He did not.

Theodore Roosevelt had won his election on a huge wave of popularity, something never before seen in the United States before. When the election of 1908 came along, he was ready to support and endorse his successor, William Howard Taft.

Chapter Eight

Post-Presidency

"Believe you can and you're halfway there."

—Theodore Roosevelt

William Howard Taft had been Roosevelt's Secretary of War and envoy to the Philippines. Taft was determined to run the country just like Roosevelt had done. At first Taft retained most of Roosevelt's cabinet members. As things go, he quickly realized he would be better served with his own hand-picked appointees.

So, Taft began replacing members of his cabinet with his own choices. This angered Roosevelt, who thought he should have been consulted. With that, Theodore took off for the African continent.

In today's ecologically-conscious atmosphere, what Roosevelt did then would be most unacceptable in our time. He was on safari with his son Kermit, and while in Africa, Roosevelt "bagged" over 3000 trophies or animals. He personally took down elephants, hippos, lions and even rhinos.

Roosevelt and his hunting party landed in Kenya and then proceeded along the Nile River to modern Sudan. The hunting expedition was looking for specimens for the

Smithsonian Institution in Washington D.C. and the American Museum of Natural History in New York.

Along the way Roosevelt met up with other renowned hunters and many land-owning families as well as having the opportunity to meet with many local leaders and native peoples. In 1907 Roosevelt became a lifelong member of the National Rifle Association. As he had done many times before, Roosevelt wrote all about his excursions in a book entitled African Game Trails.

After his experiences on safari, Theodore met up with his wife Edith in Egypt, where the two of them went on to Europe where they became the toast of the town, literally. Everyone from royalty on down wanted to meet the Roosevelts.

When Theodore and Edith returned to New York City in 1910, they were met by one of the largest receptions ever given for two people. During these last years of the Taft presidency, Roosevelt kept his opinions mostly to himself. Many of Roosevelt's friends made no secret they were less than enthusiastic about the Taft presidency.

About this time, too, Progressivism was making its way from local and state prominence onto the national stage as well. It seemed that more and more people wanted the federal government to take charge of its everyday citizens. They argued that not enough was being done for the welfare of all people. What was needed was a president who would stand up for them once again.

Chapter Nine

Election of 1912 and Final Years

"Far and away the best prize that life has to offer is the chance to work hard at work worth doing."

—Theodore Roosevelt

There's no such thing as never saying never. Once Roosevelt and his family were home once again, friends were constantly reminding him of how President Taft was undoing much of Roosevelt's political legacy. It was the Progressive wing of the Republican Party that wanted Roosevelt to challenge Taft in the election of 1912.

Roosevelt thought about it for a while then decided to throw his hat into the ring. Rather than endorse Taft as the man he once thought of as his protégé, Roosevelt actually said he felt sorry for the man. "I am sure he means well, but he means well feebly, and he does not know how! He is utterly unfit for leadership and this is a time when we need leadership," Roosevelt is quoted as saying.

The Bull Moose Party

Believing himself the savior of the Republican Party, Theodore Roosevelt declared himself a candidate. By the time the GOP met in Chicago in June of 1912 for the Convention, Republicans were split between supporters for President Taft and for the Roosevelt Progressives.

Roosevelt had won a number of primaries that had put him ahead in the delegate count. But President Taft controlled the convention. Taft's backers would not recognize Roosevelt delegates, so they were not counted. This enraged Roosevelt backers and Theodore would not allow himself to be nominated. He withdrew from the Republican Convention.

Not to be outdone, Teddy Roosevelt appeared in Chicago once again two weeks later. There he and his supporters formed the Progressive Party. Roosevelt was nominated as their candidate for president and Governor Hiram Johnson of California was nominated as his running mate. When Roosevelt stood before his convention and made his speech, he absolutely electrified his constituents. Roosevelt said he felt "as strong as a bull moose" and hence, the new name of his party was born; the Bull Moose Party.

The Bull Moose Party was working for a New Nationalism. Beliefs of the new party included political justice, an eight-hour workday, a federal securities commission, a social security system, economic opportunity for all, direct election of U.S. Senators, and a minimum wage for women.

Many of these beliefs are still prevalent today in one form or another. But Theodore Roosevelt wanted people, the citizens, to be more in control of their government. He believed that a minority, namely politicians, always held the power over everyone else. This new way would pave the way to more equality for all.

Meanwhile, Woodrow Wilson, the governor of New Jersey, had been nominated by the Democrats. Wilson like Roosevelt was also a Progressive, yet both men differed in the ways and how government would and should intervene and regulate the economy and the states.

Assassination Attempt

In 1912 while out campaigning in Milwaukee, Wisconsin, Roosevelt was shot by a saloonkeeper. The bullet came to rest in his chest after passing through his eyeglass case and through a copy of the speech he was preparing to make on that day. Fifty pages folded over once probably saved his life.

Unbelievably Roosevelt actually delivered his speech with blood dripping from his shirt before heading to the hospital. He had self-diagnosed his condition as not life-threatening; something he had learned from all his outdoor adventures. After speaking for 90 minutes and telling his audience "it takes more than that to kill a Bull Moose," Roosevelt headed to the hospital. The bullet had lodged in chest muscle and was never surgically removed.

Roosevelt carried it with him for the rest of his life. Because the bullet wasn't removed it prevented Theodore from resuming his strenuous exercise routines and he quickly became obese.

Roosevelt lost his bid for another term as president. He failed to gather enough votes for a third ticket and Woodrow Wilson was elected as the Democratic candidate.

South American Expedition

Roosevelt didn't sit still for long after the election defeat. With the backing of the American Museum of Natural History, Theodore joined a new expedition that would take him through the wilds of South America. There were new animal specimens to be found and new tropical regions to explore. It was perfect for Theodore Roosevelt.

Once the expedition found themselves in South America they decided to add one more discovery to their agenda: to find the headwaters of the Amazon River. This meant going through the Rio da Duvida, or the River of Doubt, as it was known. This river traveled north to the Madeira River which connected with the Amazon.

The trip began in late 1913 and was still going into February of 1914. While traveling on the river, Roosevelt sustained a minor leg wound from jumping into the waters attempting to stop two canoes from colliding into rocks. The leg wound soon gave him a tropical fever similar to the malaria he had suffered in Cuba years before. Because the bullet from the assassination attempt had never been removed, his health worsened.

Roosevelt stayed with the expedition, but was constantly attended to by his son Kermit and one of the physicians round the clock. After about six weeks, Roosevelt couldn't walk because of his injured leg, had been fighting high fevers, chest pains and delirium. Roosevelt even pleaded to be left behind while the rest of the expedition went on without him. His son convinced the party to include Roosevelt.

The expedition proceeded along slowly because of all the map making that had to be done. There were regular stops all along the way, which most likely saved Roosevelt's life. Once Roosevelt returned to New York, family and friends were shocked to see that he had lost about 50 pounds. He looked like a man who had been fighting for his life.

Amazingly he survived, but wrote to a friend that he feared this trip had probably cut his life short by ten years. He couldn't know how right he would be. From that point until his death, Roosevelt suffered endless bouts of malaria and leg infections that would require surgery.

Critics, of course, couldn't believe that a man in Roosevelt's physical condition could have ever completed a journey of more than 625 miles navigating a completely uncharted course. They believed he and his expedition had made it all up. Once Roosevelt was feeling better, he organized a convention in Washington D. C. With the help of the National Geographic Society and his maps,

Roosevelt successfully defended his claims as to what the expedition had accomplished.

World War I

1914 also held other surprises. In August the conflict that would become known as World War I began. Initially, President Wilson was determined through his policy of neutrality, that the United States would not get involved in the overseas struggle. Most Americans, at first, supported this idea.

Roosevelt on the other hand was highly critical of Wilson's neutrality pledge. He demanded that the administration take a hard line against Germany, particularly where submarine warfare was concerned. Roosevelt strongly supported the Allies, Britain, France, and Russia.

Theodore Roosevelt spoke out angrily about the atrocities going on in Belgium and of Americans' rights being violated in Europe. Belgium had been guaranteed neutrality under the Treaty of London, which had been signed decades before. Germany ignored any such neutrality agreement and invaded the Low Country anyway.

Once invasion began, German troops committed numerous atrocities against Belgium's civilians. In 1914 alone, 6,000 Belgians were killed and over 25,000 homes in more than 800 towns were destroyed by German forces. Throughout the war, Germany killed over 27,000 Belgian civilians. Another 70,000 died as a direct result of no food, water or shelter.

This became known as the "Rape of Belgium", and it enraged Theodore Roosevelt. In 1916 while campaigning for a Republican politician from New York, Charles Evans Hughes, Roosevelt denounced Irish-Americans and German-Americans, whom he called unpatriotic, as they supported their home countries' neutrality positions ahead of America's. He classified this behavior as traitorous to America.

Theodore Roosevelt always believed that in order to be 100% American you could not be a "hyphenated" American. He believed that if you come to America, you leave your native country behind you, including its politics.

Once news of the atrocities in Belgium spread - and the the sinking of the ocean liner Lusitania in May of 1915 - American citizens began to change their minds about staying out of the war. During these years, President Wilson was making large loans to France and Britain but had not committed any troops. He also enlarged the U.S. Navy.

In the year 1917, Germany decided to once again aggressively pursue all-out submarine warfare in the Atlantic Ocean. The Germans were targeting every commercial vessel they could find for destruction. In a summons to Mexico, called the Zimmermann Telegram, Germany asked that nation to join them.

Between fending off German submarines (also known as U-boats) and this latest act of aggression, Wilson was hard-pressed to declare which was worse. At this point, German subs began sinking American vessels in the Atlantic Ocean. Finally, on April 6, 1917 Congress declared war on Germany. Several months later on December 7, Congress additionally declared war on the Austro-Hungarian empire. Once the United States entered the war, all four of Roosevelt's sons volunteered to serve. It was a proud moment for the former president.

Just before war was declared in the United States, Congress had given former president Roosevelt authority to raise four divisions of his Rough Riders. However, President Wilson would not send Roosevelt or his volunteers to Europe. In their place he organized an American Expeditionary Force which would be headed up by General John J. Pershing.

The Rough Riders went nowhere. They were forced to disband. Because of this Roosevelt never forgave Wilson. In response he wrote and published a book entitled The Foes of Our Own Household, severely criticizing President Wilson. In the book, Roosevelt wrote that "we are in the war. But we are not yet awake" and "It is not our alien enemies who are responsible for our complete unpreparedness. It is the foes of our own household." Stinging words, to be sure, and Roosevelt meant every one of them.

Because of Roosevelt's attacks against the president, Congress was able to return to a Republican majority in 1918. Things seemed to be looking up and the war would be over soon. Yet, in July 1918 Roosevelt's youngest son Quentin, who was a pilot with the American forces in

France, was shot down behind German lines and killed. He was 20 years old. Theodore Roosevelt would never recover from this brutal loss.

With the new year of 1919, Roosevelt was in poor health. He suffered breathing problems just like he had when he was a youngster. On the night of January 5, 1919 he had seen his physician and actually felt better when heading to bed. Seeing his servant James Amos, Roosevelt politely said to him, "please put out that light, James".

Theodore Roosevelt died in his sleep that night. It was discovered that a blood clot had detached from a vein and traveled to his lungs. His son Archibald declared that "the old lion is dead". There was a private funeral at Sagamore Hill, Roosevelt's beloved homestead on Long Island. Roosevelt's burial plot is on a hillside overlooking the Oyster Bay that he so loved.

Conclusion

"A just war is in the long run far better for a man's soul than the most prosperous peace."

—Theodore Roosevelt

Theodore Roosevelt was a true Renaissance man, someone who was talented at just about everything he touched and someone who embodied the absolute epitome of what that talent should be. Roosevelt said it best when he declared, "if a man has a decided character, has a strongly accentuated career, it is normally the case of course that he makes ardent friends and bitter enemies."

America was a changing nation in the opening years of the 20th century. Whether those changes set the country on its one and true path is best debated by historians, but one thing is certain; Theodore Roosevelt loved a good fight. Whether the battles he fought were on hallowed ground, in the esteemed halls of Congress or before the Supreme Court, Roosevelt believed in those battles with all his heart.

Interesting Facts about Theodore Roosevelt

· Roosevelt was the first sitting president to leave the country. Up until this time, no president had ever made a trip outside of the United States, but in November 1906, Roosevelt traveled to the Panama Canal to personally inspect the ongoing construction.

· Roosevelt was a prolific author. Besides doing all the things he did during his lifetime, Theodore also authored 38 books, many of them detailing his adventures in Africa and South America.

· He witnessed the Abraham Lincoln funeral procession. In April 1865, a young Teddy watched from a window in his grandfather's mansion in New York City as the procession rolled by.

· Roosevelt was the father of the modern U.S. Navy. From the time Theodore was 23 years old and wrote his first book on the War of 1812, he had been obsessed with naval power. He was undersecretary of the Navy when the conflict with Cuba commenced, he sent the U.S. Navy on its worldwide tour known as the White Fleet in 1907 to show the world the power of the United States, and he built the Panama Canal.

· Theodore and Franklin Roosevelt were fifth cousins. Eleanor Roosevelt was Theodore's niece.

· Theodore was blind in one eye after a boxing injury in the White House. In 1908, he suffered a detached retina and stopped boxing as a result.

Teddy Bear Legacy

Have you ever wondered how the "Teddy" bear got its name? Well, it all started with a hunting trip in Mississippi. Other members of the hunting party were spotting bears for the kill but Roosevelt had no luck. So they tied an old bear to a tree so Roosevelt's hunting trip would look like a success. However, Roosevelt refused to shoot the bear.

Because the bear was old and injured, Theodore had someone else shoot it instead. Word of this got out to the newspapers and cartoons started appearing showing the president refusing to shoot down a tied-up bear. A Brooklyn NY shopkeeper by the name of Morris Michtom, took two stuffed bears his wife had made and put them in his shop window. Michtom asked permission of President Roosevelt if he could call these bears "teddy bears." The bears were so mass-produced that Michtom eventually formed the Ideal Novelty and Toy Company.

A German company by the name of Stieff also ended up making teddy bears. As a result, Theodore Roosevelt became well known across the globe - and his "teddy bears" have all been loved by children for generations.

Mt. Rushmore

If you travel to the Black Hills of South Dakota, you'll see a most curious site carved into the hills there. It is Mt. Rushmore, a granite formation of four of our most famous presidents. Here you will see the faces of George Washington, Thomas Jefferson, Theodore Roosevelt and Abraham Lincoln.

Now, most people would have no trouble understanding why Washington, Jefferson and Lincoln would be included on such a monument. But, why Theodore Roosevelt? Weren't there other presidents just as influential?

The four faces of these past presidents were sculpted into the granite between the years 1927 and 1941. By this time, there were many presidents to choose from. So, just what made TR, also known as Teddy Roosevelt, that fourth one to be included?

The sculptures were presided over by one Gutzon Borglum. He selected these four presidents because of their individual roles in preserving the Republic and expanding its territory. Borglum was already a famous sculptor who had carved portraits of Robert E. Lee, Thomas "Stonewall" Jackson and Jefferson Davis into Stone Mountain in Georgia. Borglum went to South Dakota to seek bigger glory.

Borglum believed there was a method he could use to carve the faces of four presidents into the mountain itself. He chose Washington, Jefferson, Lincoln and Roosevelt because each of them represented a piece of American dynasty and destiny. George Washington had been at the head of American independence in 1776, Jefferson was the author of the Declaration of Independence and expanded the country through the Louisiana Purchase, and Lincoln had preserved the Union during the Civil War.

Why was Theodore Roosevelt selected? Why didn't those who envisioned Mt. Rushmore just leave it at three sculptures and not four?

Borglum had known Theodore Roosevelt personally, some argue that he felt pressure or guilt to include him in the mix. Roosevelt had displayed a bust of Lincoln that Borglum had sculpted in the White House while he was president and in return Borglum had campaigned for Roosevelt.

However, to think this wouldn't be right. Borglum, along with many others, recognized in Theodore Roosevelt a man who was truly an extraordinary human being. American myth is a powerful entity; a man like Roosevelt is well ensconced in those hallowed halls.

Theodore Roosevelt was a man who did many things in his lifetime. From his early beginnings to rising politically and holding various offices right up to the presidency, Roosevelt did what few men have ever done. Add to that his extraordinary personal life; one of adventure, expeditions, writing, and more, many came to see how Teddy Roosevelt embodied the very best of what it meant to be an American.

Borglum and others saw in Roosevelt a president who had been a hero of the Spanish-American War, who upheld America's Manifest Destiny, the builder of the Panama Canal, a naturalist, rancher and explorer who never let anything get in his way. When Borglum was creating the Mt. Rushmore monument, Roosevelt had only been dead less than twenty years and his influence was still being felt far and wide by many who had known him personally.

One thing can be said for all four of these presidents: American power was made greater not only at home but in the world at large. America was a powerful country that didn't shy from reminding the world of her power.

That greatness came in the form of many guises. It could be as small a gesture as staking out land in the West, larger still by seeking state political offices such as governor, or it could be the epitome of power when all that the United States stood for was shadowed in the man who led the country as president. Nobel Prize winner, Rough Rider, expeditionary partner, rancher, husband, father, son; Roosevelt had been all these things not only for himself but for a country he loved most of all.

Extraordinary is a powerful word, yet it doesn't give justice to the mind of a man like Theodore Roosevelt. You might say Theodore Roosevelt was the most interesting man ever to be President of his country. That is his final and best legacy.

Made in the USA
Columbia, SC
27 May 2017